LIFE ON THE HOME FRONT WWII
Lost Words

FIONA MACDONALD

ticktock

KEY TO IMPORTANT ARTICLES

Look out for the following symbols through this book, highlighting key articles from the past.

FILM EXCERPT
Primary source material taken from
a film about the subject matter.

SONG/POEM
Lyrics extracted from songs about
the subject matter.

OFFICIAL SPEECH
Transcribed words from official
government speeches.

GOVERNMENT DOCUMENT
Text extracted from an official
government document.

LETTER
Text taken from a letter written
by a participant in the events.

PLAQUE/INSCRIPTION
Text taken from plaques/monuments
erected to remember momentous
events described in this book.

INTERVIEW/BOOK EXTRACT
Text from an interview/book by
somebody there at the time.

NEWSPAPER ARTICLE
Extracts taken from newspapers
of the period.

TELEGRAM
Text taken from a telegram sent to
or by a participant in the events.

Copyright © ticktock Entertainment Ltd 2009
First published in Great Britain in 2009 by ticktock Media Ltd.,
The Old Sawmill, 103 Goods Station Road, Tunbridge Wells, Kent, TN1 2DP
ISBN 978 1 84696 900 3 pbk
Printed in China

CONTENTS

INTRODUCTION

INVASION ROUTES

GREATER GERMANY
SOVIET UNION

0   100
Miles

BALTIC SEA · LITHUANIA · LATVIA · KOVNO · VILNA · MINSK · KOENIGSBERG · DANZIG · EAST PRUSSIA · GRODNO · NAREW · BIALYSTOK · SOVIET UNION · BERLIN · GREATER GERMANY · POZNAN · WARTA · WARSAW · VISTULA · BREST-LITOVSK · LODZ · LUBLIN · KOVEL · POLAND · KRAKOW · LVOV

GERMAN FORCES INVADED POLAND SEPTEMBER 1, 1939

SOVIET UNION OCCUPIED EASTERN POLAND SEPTEMBER 7, 1939

PROTECTORATE OF BOHEMIA AND MORAVIA · SLOVAKIA · HUNGARY · ROMANIA

Above Map showing the routes used in the successful invasion of Poland, which led to Britain's declaration of war against Germany in 1939.

B etween 1939 and 1945, the world was at war. It was a truly terrible conflict, causing more slaughter and suffering than ever before. Over 50 countries were caught up in the fighting; many others were indirectly involved.

World War II broke out in 1939 between the Allies (Britain and France) and Germany. By 1940 Germany had been joined by Japan and Italy. Together, the three were known as the 'Axis' powers. They were supported by Romania, Hungary, Slovakia, Bulgaria, Croatia and Finland. Spain, Portugal and Switzerland did not fight, but helped Germany. The Allies were aided by their colonies in India, southern Africa, the Caribbean, Canada, Australia and New Zealand.

In the early days of the war, Joseph Stalin, the leader of the Soviet Union (USSR) had signed a non-aggression pact with Adolf Hitler, the Chancellor of Nazi Germany. By the terms of this pact, each country agreed not to invade the other. When Germany broke the pact by invading the Soviet Union in 1942, the Soviet Union joined with the Allies against Germany. At first, the United States was neutral, but became a welcome, and powerful, member of the Allies following the attack by Japan on the US naval base at Pearl Harbor, Hawaii, on 7 December, 1941. China aided the United States, and was invaded by Japan.

World War II was also the first time when large-scale attacks on ordinary civilians were deliberately planned – they suffered over half the deaths and injuries of the war. Targeting civilians

Left British prime minister Winston Churchill (1874-1965) encourages civilians with his famous V-for-Victory salute.

in this way was against international law, but many governments ignored this fact in their desperate struggle to win.

German air-raids on London, known as the 'Blitz', had military goals, but were also designed to wear down Britain's will in the earliest stages of the war. Likewise, in the last months of the war the fire-bombings of Dresden, Germany, and Tokyo, Japan, killed hundreds of thousands of civilians as the Allies tried to end further Axis resistance. The final blow to Japan came in August 1945. Shortly after Germany had surrendered, the United States dropped the atomic bomb on the Japanese cities of Hiroshima and Nagasaki. Hundreds of thousands were injured and killed in the attacks, many dying later of radiation sickness in weeks and months following the raids. The will of Japan was finally broken. The Japanese government surrendered only days later.

Above *German dictator Adolf Hitler (1889-1945) receives a thunderous welcome from crowds at a Nazi rally in 1938.*

Below *Children wait anxiously amid the ruins of their demolished home after a Nazi bombing raid on London, England, 1940.*

Above *Patriotic pin displaying a defiant wartime slogan and the flags of two Allied nations, Britain and the United States.*

INTRODUCTION

Above *Polish Jews in the Warsaw ghetto c. 1942.*

Below *The entrance to the concentration camp at Auschwitz-Birkenau. It is estimated that between 1.1 and 1.5 million people died here between 1940 and 1945.*

However, the Nazis' most deliberate plans for persecution, imprisonment, deportation, and finally extermination – were aimed at Europe's Jewish population.

No-one knows precisely how many civilians were killed, but historians estimate that at least 35 million civilians died on the home front. Maybe 100 million more were injured. The largest numbers of civilians died in the Soviet Union (between 7–8 million), China (over 7.5 million), the Indian subcontinent (around 4 million) and mainland Europe, where about 6 million Jews and an approximately equal number of other civilians perished. The systematic extermination of Europe's Jews has come to be known as the 'Holocaust'.

Hitler's Nazi regime murdered millions of civilians as part of their plan to rid Europe of people they deemed social outcasts, political enemies, or threats to the Nazis' vision of a racially 'pure' German state throughout Europe. Communists, homosexuals, people with disabilities – were singled out as 'undesirable' and were systematically imprisoned or killed by the Nazis. Other civilian populations, such as Roma (Gypsies), Poles, Russians, and other Slavic peoples were thought racially inferior and persecuted or killed.

In Britain, about 90,000 civilians were killed, in France around 350,000, and in Germany at least 880,000. So, why did so many people die? Partly, because of new technology. By the 1940s, engineers had designed planes that could carry heavy loads of bombs long distances very quickly. Between 1940 and 1945, more than 30,000 bombers were built in the United States alone.

It was now possible to cause massive devastation in a single raid.

In Asia, around three million men and women were forced into slavery by Japanese invaders. Most of them died. Japan was also the only country to use biological weapons, killing over 200,000 Chinese civilians by bombing their homes with the germs of deadly diseases.

War disrupted normal life and millions of civilians ran short of food, or starved. The worst famine caused by the war was in Bengal (now Bangladesh and north eastern India) where it is estimated that 1.5 million people died. Throughout Eastern Europe and the USSR, ruthless Soviet Premier, Joseph Stalin killed around five million of his own citizens and many more in neighbouring countries. He exploited the chaos of war to get rid of his political enemies, and also to grab more land.

Soldiers and workers from the Allied nations including the United States and Britain left

home, sometimes for years, to fight and die thousands of kilometres away. War placed great strain on civilian families, as parents, children, husbands and wives were parted. Many servicemen died without seeing their babies, and millions of children never knew their fathers.

Above An American soldier says goodbye to his wife and baby in Pennsylvania station. Will he ever see them again?

Right 'We can do it!' With American men gone off to war in Europe and the South Pacific, female workers became proud of their new wartime skills when they were called on to take up jobs left vacant on the home front.

CHAPTER 1

EARLY HISTORY WAR CLOUDS OVER EUROPE

Above *Nazi poster, accusing Jewish people of betraying Germany and picturing them lurking behind the flags of Britain, the US, and the USSR. The slogan reads: 'Behind enemy powers... the Jew!'*

Below *Well armed, well trained German troops, a symbol of Hitler's wish to re-build German power, on the march in 1936.*

*O*n 10 February 1933, Adolf Hitler, the new Chancellor of Germany, broadcast a speech in front of his Nazi (National Socialist) Party supporters crowded into the vast sports stadium at Berlin. Amid shouts of 'Heil!' and 'Germany Awake!', he outlined his plans for a new and glorious nation. Germany would be reborn! Its pride would be restored, through will-power, strength and unity!

NEW HOPE
To millions of Germans, Hitler's speech offered hope and excitement, and a way to escape from what he called 'the dirt of the past 14 years'. Life for German people had not been easy since Germany's defeat in 1918 at the end of World War I. The victorious nations had forced Germany to disband its armed forces, give up land it had conquered, and pay vast sums for the damage it had caused. As a result, German industries collapsed and German currency became worthless – leaving the German people feeling humiliated.

ECONOMIC CRISIS
Germany's problems increased during the Great Depression that began in 1929. Shops and factories closed; over 5 million workers lost their jobs. German people were hungry, angry, resentful.

They no longer trusted their government, and began to look for new leaders with new ideas, to make their nation great again. They chose Adolf Hitler.

SCAPEGOATS
Unhappy Germans also looked for 'enemies of the state' to blame for their problems. They accused communists, and minority groups such as homosexuals and atheists. Most of all, they blamed the Jews. For over 100 years, Jewish families had played a leading part in German business, education, science and the arts. Yet in Germany – and much of Christian Europe – they were often treated with suspicion and disdain.

> "A state which in this age of racial poisoning dedicates itself to the care of its best racial elements must some day become lord of the earth."
>
> **Adolf Hitler, Mein Kampf [My Struggle], Volume 2.**

ATTACKS ON JEWS

Hitler claimed that Jewish people 'poisoned' Germany. He said that the nation could not unite and grow strong again unless they were removed, along with other 'outsiders' such as Slav and Roma people. So, from 1933, Jews living in Germany faced discrimination and violence. Jewish teachers, doctors and lawyers were dismissed; Jewish businesses were closed down or vandalised. About half the Jews in Germany left their country; many went to the United States. Others sent their children abroad to safety – and never saw them again.

> "Hitler came to power in 1933 . . . gradually, various problems arose. A difference was made between Aryan* and non-Aryan children. The non-Aryan - Jewish - children were told one day to sit at the back of the class. . . . The non-Jewish girls had to join the Hitler Youth . . . they were taught all kinds of anti-Semitic [anti-Jewish] things and began to hate their old friends. I was hurt and puzzled. I had not changed, so why were they not my friends any more? Gradually, only the Jewish girls were my friends.
>
> *Susan Landsman, a young Jewish girl in Nuremberg, Germany remembers the Nazi persecutions.*
> **'Aryan' was a word used by the Nazis to describe people they imagined to be ideal ethnic Germans. It has no scientific meaning.*

GREATER GERMANY

As well as rebuilding the German nation, Hitler also wanted a Nazi empire: 'Greater Germany'. He planned to create this by retaking land that Germans had occupied during World War I, and by conquering *Lebensraum* (living space) in Eastern Europe for 'Aryan' Germans. In 1935, Hitler recruited half a million soldiers, and ordered German factories to start making planes, weapons, tanks and warships. He established state building schemes and countryside work camps. With this he aimed to end unemployment and teach German people his Nazi ideas.

HITLER'S FRIENDS

In 1936, Hitler's Nazi troops took up positions in the Rhineland, a part of Germany on the border with France. In 1938, he invaded Austria, the land where he was born, and forced an *anschluss* (union) with Germany. At the same time, Hitler offered support to Francisco

Left *Adolf Hitler c. 1936. Hitler appealed to the feelings of anger common in Germany after the losses suffered in the wake of its defeat in World War I.*

TIMELINE
1933-1938

30 JANUARY 1933
Adolf Hitler becomes Chancellor of Germany.

10 MAY 1933
Nazi students burn books by Jewish writers, including Albert Einstein and Sigmund Freud.

30 JUNE 1934
Hitler gets rid of rival Nazi leaders during the 'Night of the Long Knives'.

15 SEPTEMBER 1935
Nuremberg Laws define Jews as a 'race'. They remove citizenship, marriage rights – and human dignity – from Jewish people in Germany.

30 SEPTEMBER 1938
In exchange for assurances of peace, British Prime Minister Neville Chamberlain signs the Munich Agreement to not challenge Germany's claims to parts of Czechoslovakia.

5 OCTOBER 1938
Passports belonging to German Jews must be stamped with a large red 'J'.

9 NOVEMBER 1938
Over 7,500 German Jews and Jewish businesses are attacked on 'Kristallnacht' ('Night of Broken Glass').

Above *Sir Oswald Mosley, leader of the British Union of Fascists, is met by supporters in East London.*

Below *Front cover of the* Daily Express *newspaper after the Munich Agreement of 30 September 1938.*

Franco and Benito Mussolini, the rulers of Spain and Italy. They shared his fascist aim to build mighty, warlike, unified – and intolerant – nations led by powerful, warlike dictators. Mussolini would become a military and political ally of Hitler throughout most of the war, until he was replaced by members of his own Fascist party in 1943. He was executed by Italian partisans (resistance fighters) in 1945. Franco's Spain managed to remain officially neutral during World War II, but Franco received support from both Hitler and Mussolini in his overthrow of the Spanish government during the Spanish Civil War (1936-1939), a conflict marked by incredible violence. Thanks largely to the support of Hitler and Mussolini, Franco became the dictator of Spain.

INNOCENT VICTIMS

In 1936, German planes caused outrage by bombing peaceful civilians in the Spanish town of

Guernica. However, Hitler's tough tactics also won admiration. In Britain, Sir Oswald Mosley MP led mobs of fascist citizens on violent marches through the East End of London, where Jewish families lived. In Japan, the warlike,

Right *Two Axis leaders shake hands. Hitler (right) greets Italian dictator Mussolini (left).*

Above Spanish artist Pablo Picasso (1881-1973) created a violent, anguished painting to express his shock and horror at the bombing of Guernica, in Spain.

1 DEC 1938 – 14 MAY 1940
Jewish parents in Germany, Austria and Czechoslovakia send children to safety in Britain and the US.

22 MAY 1939
'Pact of Steel' (war alliance) between Germany and Italy.

19 AUGUST 1939
Germans send U-boats to blockade the seas around Britain.

23 AUGUST 1939
Hitler makes non-aggression pact with communist USSR.

24 AUGUST 1939
Britain calls up army reservists. British government takes on emergency powers.

ultra-nationalistic government began, like Hitler, to conquer lands in order to build an empire.

APPEASEMENT

Hitler's rise to power and the growth of Germany's armed forces were deeply worrying to many European governments, especially Britain and France. For most of the 1930s, they were anxious not to quarrel with Hitler before their own troops were ready. They prepared for war, while trying to appease Germany. At that point, Britain felt it could best protect its own safety by giving in to Hitler on certain issues – and so calm down the threat he posed to Britain. In September 1938, Hitler and British Prime Minister Neville Chamberlain met in Munich, Germany. Hitler promised peace in return for the Sudetenland, an area in Czechoslovakia where many German-speaking people lived. This pact known as the Munich Agreement - was blackmail, but Chamberlain agreed not to challenge Hitler's territorial claims.

> "… In the history of our people the year 1938 will be a great, incomparable, proud year.... Later historians will show that the German nation found its way back again to the position of an honourable great nation — that our history has once more become a worthy history."

Speech by Adolf Hitler soon after signing the Munich Agreement.

Right *An Anderson shelter with bunks to sleep up to seven people. With steel walls and only cloth for a door, the shelters were difficult to sleep in. They were also damp and tended to flood, so many people risked sleeping in their homes.*

Below *3 September 1939. In New York, a newsboy holds up a paper announcing the declaration of war on Germany.*

HITLER ADVANCES

Just six months after signing the Munich Agreement, Hitler broke his promise of peace with Britain. In March 1939, he sent his army to occupy the rest of Czechoslovakia. Shortly later, his ally, Italy's Mussolini, invaded Albania. Clearly, Britain's policy of 'appeasement' was not working.

WAR IS DECLARED

On 1 September 1939, German troops attacked Poland, one of Britain's close allies. Two days later, backed by France, Prime Minister Chamberlain issued an ultimatum: 'unless...they [the Nazis] were prepared at once to withdraw their troops from Poland, a state of war would exist between us.' Hitler's army did not retreat. Britain and France declared war against Germany on 3 September 1939.

GETTING READY

The war with Germany was announced to British civilians in a radio broadcast on 3 September 1939. Some felt frightened or sorrowfully remembered the dreadful loss of life in World War I. Others were keen to 'have a go' at Hitler and his Nazis. But no-one was really surprised. For the past two years, the British government had been preparing its citizens to face enemy attackers. Precautions against air-raids included deep trenches dug in parks and playing fields and around two million iron Anderson shelters, built in British streets and gardens. They were named after John Anderson, the man charged with air raid safety by British prime minister, Neville Chamberlain.

Above *Members of the British Home Guard (volunteer defence force) practice fighting with bayonets, 1941.*

TIMELINE
1939

1 SEPTEMBER 1939
Germany invades Poland.

3 SEPTEMBER 1939
German submarines sink British passenger ship *Athenia*. Britain and France declare war on Germany.

24 SEPTEMBER 1939
Food rationing begins in Germany and many other parts of Europe.

He commissioned engineer, William Patterson to design small, cheap shelters that could be built in back gardens. These were issued free to poor people living in areas expected to be bombed by German aircraft. Later, Morrison shelters – like big metal cages – were designed for use indoors.) By late 1939, government officials had distributed 44 million gas masks to British civilians, to protect everyone, even babies, from poison-gas attack.

KEEPING CONTROL

Tough security measures included individual identity cards, and a new Ministry of Information controlled the flow of news and issued government warnings or advice. Television broadcasts were stopped; newspapers could be censored. Soon after the war began, in 1940, around 25,000 'enemy aliens' - innocent civilians living in Britain, but born in enemy countries - were rounded up and put in prison

Right *This card, issued in packs of cigarettes, demonstrates how to put on a gas mask.*

camps. Around 7,000 were shipped abroad.

FIGHTING FORCES

National Service began in Britain on 2 September 1939; all men aged 18-41 could be called up to fight. Civilians outside this age range were also soon mobilised. From May 1940, around a million men were enrolled in the Local Defence Volunteers (Home Guard).

> "We shall defend our island whatever the cost may be. We shall fight on the beaches, we shall fight on the landing grounds, we shall fight in the fields and in the streets, we shall fight in the hills, we shall never surrender. "
>
> *Speech by British Prime Minister Winston Churchill, 4 June 1940.*

WILLS'S CIGARETTES

THE CIVILIAN RESPIRATOR—HOW TO ADJUST IT

CHAPTER 2

BUILD UP OCCUPIED LANDS

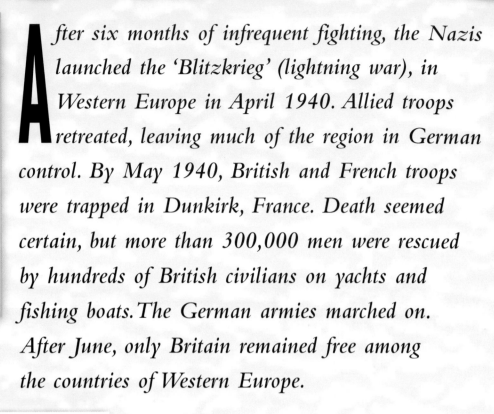

After six months of infrequent fighting, the Nazis launched the 'Blitzkrieg' (lightning war), in Western Europe in April 1940. Allied troops retreated, leaving much of the region in German control. By May 1940, British and French troops were trapped in Dunkirk, France. Death seemed certain, but more than 300,000 men were rescued by hundreds of British civilians on yachts and fishing boats. The German armies marched on. After June, only Britain remained free among the countries of Western Europe.

> "Is this the end? Has all hope vanished? Are we defeated forever? No! Believe me, I assure you that all is not lost for France. This war is not confined to our unfortunate homeland. It is a world war . . . . Whatever lies ahead, the flame of French resistance must not – and will not – be extinguished. "
>
>  **Broadcast made in Britain, 18 June 1940 by General Charles de Gaulle, leader of the Free French, whose members continued to fight Nazi occupation of France.**

Below British and French troops were rescued from the coast of Dunkirk, France, by the British military and ordinary citizens. Here, they arrive safely at Dover, England.

A LIFE OF FEAR

In occupied lands, the German conquest brought fear and chaos for civilians. German troops demanded respect, co-operation and obedience. They commandeered houses, offices, factories, transport and food supplies. They forced civilians to work on German-run factories and farms. They imposed strict curfews, forbidding people to leave their homes at night. Anyone who protested was shot. Almost everywhere, living conditions were grim, with food and fuel shortages. Hospitals and schools could not function. People lost their jobs, their houses, their farms and their families. By the end of 1940, there were over 50 million refugees in Europe – all searching for safety as the Germans advanced.

THE SEEDS OF GENOCIDE

Following Hitler's orders, thousands of men, women and children with disabilities were labelled 'unfit', then sterilised or killed. Some were subjected to brutal experiments by Nazi doctors. Tall, blonde, blue-eyed women (whom the Nazis thought looked 'Aryan') were captured and given to German officers to 'breed' more 'ideal' Germans. Much of the groundwork for these practices had been laid in Nazi propaganda and practices in the 1930s. Now - and with the

Above *French Resistance fighters hide in a civilian apartment to take shots at Nazi troops.*

building of the infamous death camp Auschwitz in Poland in June 1940 – the seeds of genocide would begin to flourish. The outlook for millions of civilians all across continental Europe was about to become a nightmare of persecution, imprisonment, enslavement, torture, and death.

RESISTANCE

Some civilians decided that the only way to survive was to collaborate with the Germans. Most just kept quiet, too scared to question or argue. But a few brave men, women and children risked their lives to fight the Nazi invaders. These people formed the many groups of fighters known collectively as the resistance. They smuggled weapons, planted bombs, cut phone and electricity cables, sabotaged factories, blew up trains, and shot at German soldiers. Fighters in the resistance spied on German tank and troop movements, set up secret transmitters, forged vital documents, sent coded messages, and worked alongside secret agents from Allied countries. They sheltered Allied soldiers trapped behind enemy lines, and helped Jewish people escape to safety.

27 SEPTEMBER 1939
British government announces new, higher, taxes to pay for war.

12 NOVEMBER 1939
Jews banned from public places in Germany.

8 JANUARY 1940
Food rationing begins in Britain.

APRIL-MAY 1940
Following the invasion of Denmark, Norway, Netherlands, Belgium, Luxembourg and France by Nazi Germany, Neville Chamberlain resigns as British Prime Minister; Winston Churchill, a vocal critic of Chamberlain's policy of 'appeasement' with Hitler and the Nazis, takes his place in office.

14 JUNE 1940
German death camp at Auschwitz, Poland, is opened.

17 JUNE 1940
General Charles de Gaulle, leader of the Free French (anti-Nazis) escapes to Britain.

Right *Fast, deadly German Messerschmitt fighter planes were used to attack the UK during the 'Battle of Britain', 1940. Germany lost and called off its planned invasion of England.*

"Her whole body was buried under the sand but she did not move until it began to cover her mouth. She was lying face upwards, breathed in some sand and started to choke, and then, scarcely realising what she was doing, she started to struggle in a state of uncontrollable panic...

With her left hand, the good one [a Nazi soldier had crushed her other hand], she started scraping the sand off herself, scarcely daring to breathe lest she should start coughing; she used what strength she had to hold the cough back.

Dina Pronicheva recounts her experience of being shot with over 30,000 other Jewish civilians at Babi Yar, Kiev, Ukraine September 1941. She survived by pretending to be dead.

INTO THE USSR

In 1939, Germany and the USSR found it useful to be at peace with each other. But in June 1941, Hitler ordered Nazi troops to invade Soviet land. As the Nazis advanced, Jews, Roma and other minority groups were massacred. As German armies besieged the three greatest Soviet cities, Leningrad, Stalingrad and Moscow, other ordinary citizens became the main target for attack. Thousands were trapped, in fear and horror. The longest siege, at Leningrad, lasted almost 900 days from September 1941 to January 1944. Homes were smashed by shells and gunfire raked the streets. Prevented by German troops from receiving food or fuel, citizens shivered in rags, eating rats, grass, wallpaper and even dead bodies in a desperate bid to survive.

THE HOLOCAUST BEGINS

Before World War II, some German Jews managed to flee Germany, or at least get their children out. There were also Jewish communities in most other European nations, and these too were beginning to come under attack as Germany extended its reach throughout Europe. The total number of Jews in Europe was not large – probably fewer than 10 million. But Hitler was determined to get rid of them all, and so Jewish civilians in Nazi-occupied lands were especially cruelly treated. By the time Germany had invaded their homelands, escape was virtually impossible. The few Jews who managed to survive usually did so by going into hiding.

IN THE GHETTO

In many cities, Jewish families were forced to live like prisoners in crowded ghettoes. These ghettoes of Nazi-occupied Europe were closed off – often behind walls – from the rest of the city. The inhabitants were usually denied basic food, medical, and social services. Thousands died of hunger, cold or disease. As the war progressed, and the campaign to

Right *German-born Jewish teenager Anne Frank (1929-1945) escaped with her family to the Netherlands, then spent two years in hiding. But she was betrayed, arrested, and taken to a concentration camp, where she died. Her diary, found after her death, became a symbol of the strength of the human spirit under even the most terrible conditions.*

Above *Nazi soldiers arrest civilians in the Jewish ghetto in Warsaw, Poland, 1942. Between July and September 1942, the Nazis shipped about 265,000 Jews from Warsaw to the death camp Treblinka.*

TIMELINE 1940

28 JUNE 1940
All foreigners in the United States must be registered and fingerprinted.

9 JULY – 31 OCTOBER 1940
Battle of Britain: German fighter planes attack UK, but fail to conquer it. Churchill praises the bravery of British pilots killed fighting the invaders: 'Never in the field of human conflict was so much owed by so many to so few.'

exterminate the Jews accelerated, the ghettoes became places where Jews might be held before they were transported to Nazi death camps. Although they suspected what their future might hold, ghetto-dwellers made huge efforts to continue normal, civilised life. They set up schools, shared food, played music, ran welfare schemes and celebrated Jewish festivals. Many ordinary men and women showed extraordinary courage, such as Dr Janus Korczak, who ran a home for orphans in the Warsaw Ghetto, Poland, and chose to be killed beside them, rather than abandon them.

NAZI MASSACRES
In Poland and the Baltic states of Estonia, Latvia, and Lithuania, Nazi *Einsatzgruppen* (death squads) travelled to each village. They looted Jewish homes and then shot the inhabitants – often making them dig their own graves beforehand. Around 1.5 million Jews were murdered in this brutal, organised manner.

Right *Jews living in Nazi-occupied lands were forced to sew badges (like this one from Holland) to their clothes, to clearly identify them.*

"Because Leningrad's water system was destroyed, children went to the river and brought up water in buckets. In winter, thousands of 'ice children' dug up ice from the river to bring home to their family. Black market food soared to unbelievable prices. Two weeks' salary were required to buy a loaf of bread."

Grim conditions endured by civilians during the Nazi siege of Leningrad (now St Petersburg) as described in a travelling exhibition about Russian experiences in World War II.

Above *Shocked civilians survey the charred ruins of a busy shopping street after a German bombing raid on the city of Coventry, England, November 1940.*

Throughout the war, the Allied and Axis powers dropped bombs on military and civilian targets. Intensive bombing raids on civilians began with the Blitz. From September 1940 until May 1941, German planes dropped explosives nightly. During the first month, over 5,300 tonnes fell on London. The bombers aimed for Britain's national institutions, such as Parliament, and its docks. However, many bombs hit houses, shops and schools.

Likewise, American British, and other Allied aircraft bombed civilian targets in Germany and Japan, particularly toward the end of the war. The purpose of these bombings was as much to demoralise the population and convince the Axis powers that defeat was inevitable as to score specific military gains.

FIRE-BOMBS AND ROCKETS

In 1940, Germany tried a new, deadly, weapon: fire-bombs. Nine hundred fell on the British city of Coventry on 14 November. On that one day alone, one-third of all the houses in Coventry were destroyed and over 550 of its residents were killed. Later, German bombers dropped huge landmines on many civilian areas. In 1944 and 1945, Germans launched unmanned V1 flying bombs and V2 rockets that flew for a fixed distance and then fell and exploded without warning. Since these could not be aimed, they were obviously designed to kill and terrorise civilians with their random attacks.

ALLIED RAIDS

To retaliate, British and American bombers made equally damaging raids on German targets. The United States bombed by day, targeting German roads, railways, bridges and industrial centres. Britain bombed at night,

Right *A German V2 rocket ready for launch, 1945. Rocket attacks were a new and terrifying kind of warfare, targeted at civilians on the home front.*

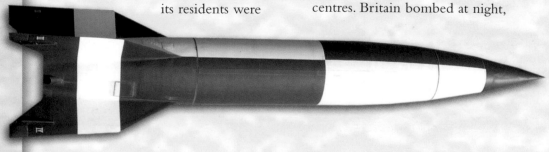

> "It [London] was on fire. The Guildhall [historic trade centre and mayor's office] was on fire. Wherever one looked up the narrow alleys of the city, you saw what looked like red snowstorms. Great showers of sparks were coming from the buildings.... I loved the city and I knew its buildings. And there I was, simply watching the whole thing burn."
>
> **Stanley Baron, newspaper reporter, describes the London Blitz.**

Above *Wartime painting showing fires caused by German bombing raids on the suburbs of London.*

striking at densely populated towns and cities sheltering troops and civilian refugees. In 1944, over 130,000 people were killed in one night when British planes fire-bombed Dresden, a city in north Germany.

AFTER PEARL HARBOR

On 7 December 1941, an early morning Japanese bombing raid on the US naval base at Pearl Harbor, Hawaii, killed or wounded 4,500 people, – nearly half of them civilians. The surprise attack caught US forces largely unprepared, despite signs that Japan had been preparing for some kind of operation against the United

> "When I was rescued, my hair was burned; my face was inflated like a balloon . . . . It was hell. I saw people looking for water and they died soon after they drank it. I saw many people go to the river in search of water and who died. The whole city was destroyed and burning. There was no place to go."
>
> **Michiko Yamaoka remembers the bombing of Hiroshima, 1945.**

States for some time. It also persuaded the United States to end its neutral status and join the war on the side of Allies. From 1942 onwards, US planes made strategic bombing raids on Japan. They used fire-bombs to devastate Tokyo, the capital city, killing 100,000 civilians in a single raid. On 6 and 9 August 1945, they dropped the world's first atomic bombs on two Japanese ports, Hiroshima and Nagasaki. Between 70,000 and 80,000 people were killed in Hiroshima, with more than 70,000 injured. In Nagasaki, between 35,000 and 40,000 people were killed, with a similar number injured. No-one had ever seen – or could have imagined – such massive explosions or so many terrible injuries. These attacks, in combination with the Soviet Union's invasion of Japanese-occupied

Right *Survivors of the atomic bombing of Hiroshima in an old bank building which had been turned into a makeshift hospital.*

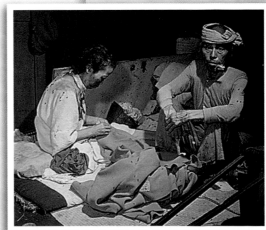

7 SEPTEMBER 1940
Start of the 'Blitz' aerial attacks on London.

4 FEBRUARY 1941
United Service Organizations (union of civilian volunteer helper groups) founded in US.

16 FEBRUARY 1941
Nazis deport 10,000 Jews from Vienna, Austria.

1 MARCH 1941
US Congress passes 'Lend-Lease' Act, to supply planes, ships and weapons to Britain and its allies.

6 APRIL 1941
'Operation Punishment': Germans bomb Belgrade, capital of Yugoslavia, for 11 days.

10 MAY 1941
End of London Blitz. Six months of bombing leaves around 40,000 civilians killed and over 80,000 badly injured.

> "When bombs were falling, I have seen big men become rooted to the spot, transfixed by terror beyond their control. I have seen others set off and run blindly in sheer panic, in no particular direction..."
>
> *Hugh Varah, Auxiliary firefighter, Hull, northern England.*

Below *An ARP (Air Raid Precautions) warden cradles a homeless child in her arms, following a German 'Baedecker' raid on the historic city of Norwich, eastern England.*

Manchuria on 9 August, proved to be too much for Japan. The war was over.

SHATTERED LIVES

During the London Blitz, newspapers and posters displayed a cheery, defiant, slogan: 'Britain can take it!'. But, in reality, bombing raids everywhere took a terrible toll. As well as many thousands of civilian deaths from blast injuries, fires and suffocation, millions more men, women and children were injured or disabled by bombs.

Countless families were traumatised by the explosions, and by homelessness, hunger, the loss of all their treasured possessions, and the breakdown of peaceful, normal, everyday life. The loss of family pets added to the misery of those whose lives had already been stripped of so much, especially children. Many pets were killed or injured; others became lost or ran away in bombing raids. People in bombed cities became depressed or prone to panic attacks, developed strange behaviours, or fell physically ill from the stress. Weeks of sleepless nights left many survivors short-tempered, forgetful, and exhausted. On top of this, grief and shock also had a deep effect on people.

CIVILIAN HELPERS

At the same time, civilians made tremendous efforts to limit the damage done by bombing raids, and to help survivors. In Britain, for example, they became ARP (Air Raid Precautions) Wardens, patrolling the streets, checking air-raid shelters and helping to rescue people from collapsed buildings. They joined teams of fire-watchers or the new Auxiliary Fire Service. Women became telephonists who worked at telephone switchboards, messengers, despatch riders, ambulance drivers and first-aid workers. They ran canteens and emergency shelters, offering food, clothes, blankets and a place to rest for bomb victims and emergency crews.

Beat FIREBOMB FRITZ

BRITAIN SHALL NOT BURN

BRITAIN'S FIRE GUARD IS BRITAIN'S DEFENCE

Above *A German fire-bomb pictured on a British government warning poster, 1940.*

LIVING WITH BLACKOUT

Civilians in many European countries – and along the north east coast of the United States had to obey strict 'Black-out' or 'Dim-out' regulations. Street lights were switched off, windows were fitted with heavy curtains, and train, lorry and car lamps were dimmed, to stop escaping light guiding German bombers towards easy targets. One city resident recalled: 'I lived near a main highway; almost every night, someone was knocked down in the dark.'

BRUTAL INVADERS

Many European, Soviet and Asian towns and cities suffered terrible damage from shells and gunfire, as well as from bombs. Civilians risked their lives in everyday activities, such as queuing for essential food supplies. Advancing or retreating troops fought their way along city streets, shooting through windows and smashing doors to hunt for enemy soldiers, while frightened men, women and children cowered in basements or hid under beds. Invading armies also brutally attacked citizens. In 1938, Japan invaded Nanking, China, killing over 360,000 civilians, and raping thousands of women. In 1944, when Japan conquered the Philippines, all males over 14 in Manila, the capital, were shot. In 1945, towards the end of the war, Soviet soldiers raped and killed thousands of German civilians, in revenge for atrocities that the Nazis had committed against Soviet civilians.

> "I didn't usually worry about air-raids, but once I was cycling home to London after a trip to the countryside. I reached the top of a hill, and saw London spread out before me. I could also see planes overhead, and searchlights, and hear anti-aircraft gunfire. I felt sure that my home would be hit by a bomb, and raced the last miles home in a panic. The nearer I got, the more certain I felt that I would find my family dead and our house in ruins!"
>
> *Geoff Field, a young boy aged 11 when the war started, remembers bombing raids on his home in south London.*

Above Civilians spend the night sheltering from German 'Blitz' bombing raids in a London Underground station, 1940.

> "I never felt scared in the blackout. I was only 18 but I left my workplace in total darkness, walked alone though unlighted city streets, and caught a dark train back to my village. Anyone could have followed me or sat next to me; you just couldn't see people's faces .... In winter, the [steam] trains were bitterly cold, as well as dark. There was barely enough coal for their fuel, and none for heating. I used to take a hot water bottle with me..."
>
> *Mary Mills, a young girl aged 16 and working at her first job in a busy town in southern England, recalls her experience of the blackout.*

TIMELINE 1941-1942

27 MAY 1941
US President Roosevelt declares a national emergency; asks all Americans to oppose Nazism.

25 JUN 1941
US Congress bans racial discrimination among arms-factory workers.

7 DECEMBER 1941
Japan attacks US naval base at Pearl Harbor, Hawaii; around nearly half of those killed are civilians.

8 DECEMBER 1941
United States declares war on Japan, then (11 December) on Germany and Italy.

DECEMBER 1941-JUNE 1942
Japan occupies Guam, Hong Kong, the Philippines, Thailand, Malaya, Singapore, Java, Borneo, Bali, Sumatra, Timor and Burma. Civilians are imprisoned, forced to labour, and starved.

> "... heavy calibre shells tore to pieces hundreds of women who were waiting in the market hall. Dead and wounded alike were flung on wheelbarrows and carried away; the surviving women continued to wait, patient, resigned, sullen, until they had finished their miserable shopping."

Claus Fuhrman, a Berlin citizen, describes how Soviet troops shelled desperate, half-starving women in the capital city of Germany, in 1945.

Above *A long queue outside the passport office in London. Many of these people were trying to find out about evacuation to Canada.*

SEEKING SAFETY – EVACUATION

To escape these horrors, children, pregnant women and nursing mothers were often evacuated from cities to country areas. This was only possible before invaders had taken control; after that, few citizens were allowed to travel freely. Even before war had actually broken out, families often made their own arrangements to stay with friends or relatives, or paid people living in the country to feed and shelter them. Some wealthy European parents sent their children far away, to South Africa, Australia, Canada or the United States.

In Britain, the government organised an official evacuation scheme. From 1 September 1939, children from big cities were assembled, labelled with their names and ages, and put on special trains or coaches supervised by teachers and female volunteers. At their destinations, they were handed over to volunteer 'host' families – strangers whose country lives were very different from their own. Evacuees and hosts alike

Right *Some children enjoyed their time as evacuees. In this photo, a country teacher drives her class of evacuated children back to the farms where they are staying.*

faced a wide range of experiences. Being evacuated – and hosting children fleeing the horrors of war – affected everyone differently, and everyone had a unique story to tell.

AWAY FROM HOME

The contrasts between urban and rural life were often difficult for both the city children and their rural hosts. Some hosts were kind and caring; others treated their evacuees very badly. Misunderstandings were common; hosts and evacuees spoke in different local accents and dialects. Middle-class families were often less willing to host city children than were working-class families. Some city children faced prejudices that came from people who weren't used to being around city people. Many hosts also had different expectations of behaviour, manners and hygiene. Understandably, many children were homesick. Others settled down happily into routines that felt safe and predictable. Many evacuees were left with happy memories and formed friendships that outlasted the war by decades.

Back in the cities, some parents worried about their children so much that they brought them home, against government advice. They preferred to risk dying together, rather than be separated. They found it easier to endure the hardships of life on the home front when surrounded by loved ones.

Below *Children playing in the major port town of Dover, England in 1941. This area came to be known as 'Hellfire Corner' because it faced so many heavy bombing raids by German planes.*

TIMELINE
1942

17 JANUARY 1942
Nazi leaders announce the so-called Final Solution – a plan to kill all Jews in Europe.

23 FEBRUARY 1942
Mutual Aid Agreement. The United States agrees to make warships, weapons and vehicles for Britain.

23 FEBRUARY 1942
Japanese submarine shells oil field near Santa Barbara, on the coast of California, US. Little damage is done, and no-one is seriously injured.

MARCH 1942
British planes bomb German Baltic Sea ports.

18 APRIL 1942
US planes bomb a number of Japanese cities.

" . . . . when I got to school, there was no morning prayers and we were given a badge to wear with a number. We were told to sit in class, everyone looking at each other but no-one told us anything. We were told to go to these old-fashioned Ford coaches and we got on them . . . . We were being evacuated. We were billeted with a family in a little village in Wales. I'd never been to the country before."

Derek Haycock remembers his childhood being evacuated to Wales in 1939.

Above On this American poster, a cheery but heroic US airman encourages civilians to join a government savings scheme by buying war bonds.

I n all countries fighting in World War II, civilians' lives were disrupted, even if their home town had not been invaded or bombed. On both sides, civilians were expected to take part in their nation's 'war effort'. Everywhere, personal freedom was severely restricted.

In Britain, for example, the right to travel, choose a job, buy clothes and food, occupy a house, read books and newspapers, listen to the radio, and talk freely in public were all controlled by government regulations. In Britain and the United States alike, this meant cutting back on wearing fashionable clothing due to the rationing of cloth and other materials. In the United States, people were urged to save cooking fat or oil drippings, put them in tin cans, and then sell or donate the fat to be used to make explosives for bombs and guns.

TAXES AND SAVINGS

Leaders worldwide reorganised national economies, controlling prices to stop traders making unfair profits from scarce goods. They collected higher taxes to pay for troops and weapons and raised extra money for war through government saving schemes. In the United States, for example,

"I worked the graveyard shift 12:00–8:00 A.M. in the shipyard. I took classes on how to weld. I had leather gloves, leather pants, big hood, goggles and a leather jacket . . . .

They put me forty feet down in the bottom of the ship to be a tacker. I filled the long seams of the cracks in the ship corners full of hot lead and then brushed them good and you could see how pretty it was. The welders would come along and weld it so it would take the strong waves and deep water and heavy weight. I liked it pretty good.

I don't remember how much I got paid for working. Lots of people came to Richmond to work in the shipyards. Lots of women went to help with the war. I told Melvin [her husband, fighting overseas] later that I helped to make a ship for him to come home in."

Katie Grant, a young, married woman, describes the skills she learned in US shipyards, making and repairing US warships.

Below *Women contribute to the war effort by driving tanks, trucks and testing guns at the army Proving Grounds.*

workers were urged to save 10 per cent of their earnings. If a whole workforce met the target their office or factory was allowed to fly a special flag.

WAR INDUSTRIES

Everywhere, industry was transformed. Factories were converted to make tanks, planes, warships, gas masks and uniforms, rather than sports kit, cosmetics or fashionable clothes. Civilian workers were ordered to stop making consumer goods such as cookers or cars and to start making weapons, or else to grow essential food products.

New mass-production methods, pioneered by Ford in the United States (automobiles and assembly lines) and Krupp in Germany (manufacturing products made out of steel), were used in wartime factories to make vast quantities of identical items such as bullets or tyres. Entire industries grew up around manufacturing clothing and other items that might otherwise not have been in such high demand. The US Army ordered over 4 million rifles, for example, and 57 million soldiers' undershirts. Because raw materials for industry were so scarce, scientists invented replacements, such as synthetic rubber. They also found new uses for everyday products – for instance, in America, peanut oil to lubricate heavy machines.

WOMEN DO MORE THAN LEND A HAND

Britain actually conscripted women into its armed services. In the United States, women's branches of the armed forces were set up by the Army and Navy. Women drove lorries and even piloted aircraft. Female pilots

Right *A woman works on the assembly line at an ammunition factory in California. The equipment is clean, and the woman's clothing is neat and attractive. These suggest that the photo was probably a wartime propaganda picture, with a bit of glamour added to publicise factory jobs for women on the home front.*

"It was a big place. My guess would be that some 30,000 workers were running three shifts and that they were making a very presentable number of airplanes each day....

More than thirty-five per cent of the labor in the plant was done by women. Among the workers we saw boys not more than ten years old ... the children work, in many of the shops [factory departments], the full sixty-hour week worked by adults."

US business and political leader (and presidential candidate in 1940) Wendell Wilkie.

TIMELINE 1942

APRIL 1942
To punish China for helping the United States, Japanese massacre 250,000 Chinese civilians.

23 APRIL – 6 JUNE 1942
'Baedecker' (tourist) raids: German planes bomb British cities famous for their fine buildings.

28 APRIL 1942
Dim-out along northeast coast of United States after German submarines approach.

15 MAY 1942
Petrol rationing begins in eastern United States.

18 MAY 1942
German student protesters put up anti-Nazi posters in Berlin. All are shot.

30 MAY 1942
Britain begins '1000-bomber' (intensive) raids on German cities.

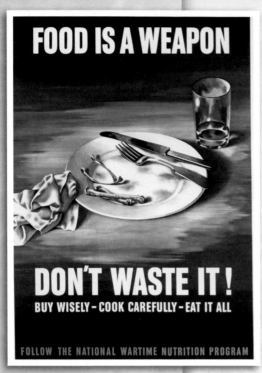

FOOD IS A WEAPON

DON'T WASTE IT!
BUY WISELY – COOK CAREFULLY – EAT IT ALL

FOLLOW THE NATIONAL WARTIME NUTRITION PROGRAM

Above In all war-torn countries, governments urged civilians to eat wisely, and not to waste food.

"…. you, too, are fighting; helping to defeat the enemy's attempt to starve us out…

..nearly half our food comes across the sea. The U-boats [German submarines] attack our food ships, and, although most arrive safely, some are lost.

Now, here is your part in the fight for Victory. When a particular food is not available, cheerfully accept something else - home produced if possible. Keep loyally to the rationing regulations."

UK Government newspaper advertisement, 1940.

did not fly in combat missions, but they helped deliver goods and supplies that were a part of the war effort. None of these roles would have been open to women were it not for the incredible need for people to manufacturer and deliver the materials of war.

As the war effort got into full gear, and increasing numbers of men were serving – and dying – on the front lines of battle, women became vital contributors in ways that had once been unthinkable. Women in Europe, Russia and the United States were recruited to work in heavy industries, replacing male workers who had been called up to fight. Women, children and prisoners were also sent to work on farms, along with conscientious objectors – citizens who refused to fight because of religious or ethical beliefs.

Below A propaganda picture showing children eating naturally sweet carrots, instead of sugary treats that were unobtainable in wartime.

ON THE MOVE

In the United States, the war led to major population changes: 27 million people moved back in with parents and other family members. Many of these were girlfriends or wives of men who were in the armed forces. Some migrated westwards, to work in docks and factories close to the Pacific. Many African-Americans left farms in the southern states for jobs in northern industries. Residents of Japanese origin, most of them born and raised in the United States as ordinary citizens, were moved away from the west coast – at gunpoint – by the US government. Less concerned with Japanese-Americans' civil rights than with the fear that they might act as spies, the government established a number of internment camps to house them for the duration of the war. The government also relocated Italian-Americans from areas on the east coast.

Above *Women in London wait in a queue, hoping to be able to buy potatoes, which although not rationed, were often in short supply.*

FAIR SHARES

As well as controlling the placement of workers, governments everywhere introduced rationing. Rationing limited the quantity of food, clothing, fuel and other essential items that any person could buy. Rationing rules applied to everyone, rich and poor. Their aim was to allow fair shares of scarce, important, supplies. Some goods were in short supply because the raw materials used to make them – such as dairy products, cotton or oil – were being redirected to feed, clothe, and transport troops and equipment in the war. Other goods, such as cars, were in short supply because the factories making them were being used to manufacture ammunition, military vehicles, and other equipment. Citizens had to prove their right to receive rationed goods. Governments issued individuals with books of coupons, and customers handed these over with their cash when making a purchase. Buying rationed items without coupons was prohibited.

RATIONING FUEL

Everywhere, coal and petrol rationing saved energy to power factories, warships and planes, transport troops and weapons, and provide a

4 oz [112 g] butter
8 oz [224 g] sugar
4 oz [112 g] bacon or ham
3 oz [84g] cheese
One egg
3 pints [1.704 litres] of milk
2 oz [56 g] tea
2 oz [56 g] cooking fat or margarine
2 oz [56 g] jam or marmalade or syrup or treacle
2 oz [56 g] sweets or chocolate
Meat, biscuits, tinned fruit, beans and meat were also strictly rationed, but bread, potatoes and other vegetables were not. Fruit, which often had to be shipped from warm climates, was scarce and expensive due to restrictions on travel and on the use of fuel and transport.

A typical week's food rations for a British adult, 1943 (Precise quantities varied from year to year.)

TIMELINE
1942-1943

MAY 1942

WAC (or WACS) (the Women's Army Corps) set up as a branch of the US Army.

7 JUNE 1942

US Navy wins Battle of Midway against Japan.

JULY 1942

WAVES (Women Accepted for Voluntary Emergency Services) organisation set up as a branch of the US Navy.

AUGUST-SEPTEMBER 1942

Japanese seaplane drops incendiary bombs on Oregon forests, US; the forest is damp and Forest Service workers are able to extinguish the blaze.

Below *A UK post wartime ration book.*

 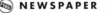

> "I had no ration coupons to buy little shoes for my bridesmaids. So I made them myself, out of left-over scraps of cloth with cardboard for the soles."
>
> *Jane Smith, a British bride at the end of the war, recalls how she solved clothes-rationing problems for her special day.*

Below *British propaganda poster. Sewing was an essential skill in wartime. Even troops were taught to mend holes in their socks.*

minimum of heating, lighting and hot water for civilians. Patriotic families in Britain drew a line around bath-tubs, 12.5 centimetres (5 inches) above the bottom, to make sure that they did not over-fill them.

PRECIOUS FOOD

Often, civilians felt frustrated by rationing, but in countries like Britain, the United States, and Canada, it guaranteed that everyone would get what they needed to survive. Perishable goods and foods imported from overseas were no longer available, so housewives learned to cook with substitutes such as dried egg, or served unfamiliar dishes, including horse meat and carrots added to cakes to replace fruit. Left-overs might be fed to animals that in turn produced food – like chickens. Or they might be collected by members of 'Pig-Clubs', who joined together to raise and fatten a pig and then share its meat between them.

In occupied countries, and also in Germany, people often went hungry and sometimes starved. In the Netherlands, there was a dreadful famine in the winter of 1944-1945. Desperate citizens tried to survive by eating daffodil and tulip bulbs.

WAR FASHIONS

Wartime clothes, hats, shoes, house furnishings and even children's toys were also affected by rationing. In Europe and the United States, clothes styles were simple and close-fitting, so as not to waste precious material. Many designs featured square shoulders and belted waists, like army jackets. Shoes were sturdy and designed to be long-lasting rather than fashionable.

Socks and women's stockings (made of fine wool, silk or cotton) were scarce; one famous UK brand was advertised as 'rarer than diamonds'. So many women wore trousers (a new, daring fashion) or siren suits. (These were all-in-one jump-suits, warm and cosy in draughty air-raid shelters.) For special occasions, smart young women covered their legs with tinted cream, although cosmetics, shampoo and perfume were all expensive luxuries. At work, women tied their hair back under nets or scarves; for parties, they tried styles with patriotic names like 'Victory Roll'. Short hair, army-style, or the American crew-cut, were the fashions for men.

RECYCLING

New clothes or shoes were a rarity. Everyone tried to 'Make-Do and Mend', by repairing or recycling existing items. Dresses and trousers were patched, sweaters featuring multi-coloured patterns were knitted from wool oddments. Hats (worn by most people in the 1940s) were often home-made, using wild bird's feathers or leaves for decoration. Children wore clothes made from cut-down adult garments; babies were dressed in cast-offs or kept warm in old blankets. Toys were

Above These British women are spinning hair combed from their dogs to make yarn, ready to knit into warm gloves, socks and scarves.

often home-made, and mostly had a wartime theme – model soldiers, planes, guns, dolls dressed as nurses, or teddy bears made of scrap fabrics. Older children liked to play in ruined buildings and bomb craters, although dangers from unstable buildings and unexploded munitions made this a very dangerous form of play.

UTILITY GOODS

Families whose homes had been bombed needed to find new furnishings. Wood was in short supply (it was used for building planes) and so were fabrics. Many families in war-torn Europe had to wait for replacements until long after the end of the war. In Britain, however, the government allowed limited quantities of basic 'utility' household items to be made, in plain, practical styles.

'DIG FOR VICTORY'

Civilians often grumbled about new wartime regulations, but they also worked hard for the war effort. In the United States, Canada, and Britain, people grew fruit and vegetables in backyards or 'Victory Gardens', and kept chickens, rabbits and goats for eggs, meat and milk. This helped all three nations save money which could be redirected towards the war effort and become more self-reliant. This was especially critical for Britain, where commercial ships bringing in food from other parts of the world were likely to be attacked by German U-boats which patrolled the waters around Britain, hoping to cut off supplies that would prolong the war.

Left A woman is dressed in a blouse and dungarees which cost very few ration stamps.

TIMELINE 1942-1944

13 SEPT 1942 – 2 FEB 1943
Germans shell and bomb Stalingrad (now Volgograd), USSR. Half a million citizens die; the survivors refuse to surrender.

1 DECEMBER 1942
Beveridge Report published in UK. It plans a new 'Welfare State' for civilians.

28 JANUARY 1943
All German adults mobilised for 'total war'.

19 APRIL 1943
Uprising by Jews in the Warsaw Ghetto.

3 SEPTEMBER 1943
Italy agrees to secret peace treaty with Britain, United States and the Allies.

25 APR 1943 – 24 JUN 1944
16,000 captured Allied troops and 80,000 Asian civilians die building Burma-Thailand railway for Japanese.

27 JULY 1943
Britain bombs German city port of Hamburg; 40,000 civilians die in one night.

1 JANUARY 1944
German schoolchildren mobilised for war work.

6 JANUARY 1944
Soviet troops advance into German-occupied Poland.

> "In the cities, and even in the country, they wanted everybody to have their own garden, to raise their own produce ...because it wasn't available in the stores...
>
> It was a great morale thing. And for young people like me, it was, you know, I could do my part. I was part of the effort."
>
> **US farmer Kelly Holthus remembers his Victory Garden.**

SURVIVAL STRATEGIES

Wild foods helped keep many civilians alive, especially in the USSR, Poland, and eastern Germany. People whose homes or farms had been destroyed were forced to scavenge in fields and forests for nettles, nuts and berries. In autumn, they gathered mushrooms and acorns. In Britain, government factories processed wild rose-hips, picked by civilian volunteers, to extract life-saving Vitamin C.

NEW FROM OLD

In Europe and the United States, schools, neighbourhoods and places of worship organised 'scrap drives' to collect different kinds of waste materials for recycling to help with the war effort. Metal toothpaste tubes, cooking pots, gates and fences were all melted and turned into planes and warships. Old paper was turned into aircraft engine gaskets and packaging for gun-cartridges.

Above *American children in Washington D.C., United States, collect scrap metal for the war-effort.*

Below *As well as sending letters to comfort troops overseas, generous civilians on the home front also gave money to charities that send food parcels to Allied prisoners-of-war.*

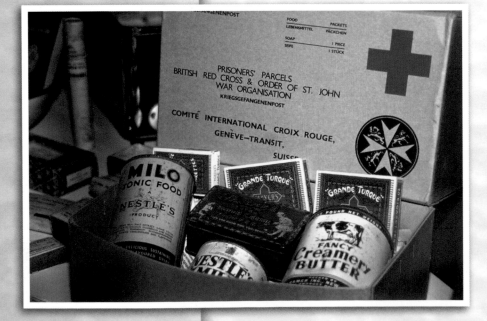

HOME COMFORTS

Civilians also helped by renting rooms to war-factory workers, walking to work or sharing cars to save petrol, and giving blood. Americans, Canadians, Australians and others living in lands that had not been invaded, showed great kindness and generosity and packed up 'Bundles for Britain' – full of useful as well as luxury items. Many women knitted warm socks and scarves for the troops, and families invited refugees to their homes. Wives, children, parents and neighbours wrote letters to cheer and comfort troops serving far away.

SHOOT TO KILL!

PROTECT YOUR VICTORY GARDEN

Left *This poster encourages everyone to take care of their Victory Garden, and grow food to feed families.*

Below *A US Navy sailor is delighted to receive a letter from 'back home'.*

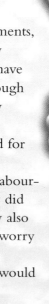

COMMUNITY SPIRIT

For people on the home front in Britain and North America alike, winning the war was considered very much a 'job' and a way of life. So along with the personal sacrifices, the frequent air-raid drills, and the threats of injury, came the sense of comradeship, patriotism, and a strengthened sense of community.

EXHAUSTED!

The civilian war effort was essential. Without it, governments, military personnel and many ordinary people would not have survived. Wartime life was tough for women, especially if they were married. They worked long hours in factories, cared for children, ran their homes – without the help of today's labour-saving machines – and many did voluntary work as well. They also lived with the terrible daily worry of wondering whether their husbands, sons and brothers would be killed fighting.

TIMELINE 1944

6 JUNE 1944
British, American and other Allied forces start D-Day invasion to recapture German-occupied France.

12 JUNE 1944
Germany sends V1 flying bombs to attack British cities.

25 AUGUST 1944
Germans retreat from Paris.

8 SEPTEMBER 1944
Germany sends larger, more powerful V2 rockets to attack Britain.

25 OCTOBER 1944
US navy destroys Japanese fleet at the Battle of Leyte Gulf.

D epending on which country they lived in – and if they were free or living under occupation – civilians on the home front had to face bombing raids, rationing, curfews, blackouts, shortages, long working hours, travel difficulties and partings from loved ones. In Britain and the United States, everyone looked forward to an occasional night out with friends. It was a chance for people to enjoy themselves and forget the war for a while.

Above *Filmgoers liked to forget their wartime worries for a while, and lose themselves in epic romances such as Gone with the Wind.*

MUSIC FOR DANCING

Big bands led by star instrumentalists, like Glen Miller from the United States, played music for ballroom dancing, the most popular entertainment among young people. In Europe and the United States, many people met their future wives or husbands at a dance. In rural areas, energetic traditional dances were also popular.

SENTIMENTAL SONGS

In between dances, glamourous solo singers might croon a romantic ballad, or sing longingly of a happy future when the war was over. Among the best-known, and best-loved, singers were Britain's Vera Lynn, 'the Forces Sweetheart' and German-born actress Marlene Dietrich, who lived and worked in the United States. Her songs were popular with Allied and Axis troops alike.

"On Saturday nights, we all liked to go dancing. We girls changed out of our working clothes and put on a dress, if we had one. Many of the men were in uniform. The dances were great fun, but also rather sad. When you said goodbye at the end of the evening, you could never be sure that you would see your dancing partners again. By next Saturday, they might have been killed in action...."

Mary Jones, a teenage girl living in wartime England, describes how a simple Saturday night out might mingle entertainment with tragedy.

Right *Marlene Dietrich, although born in Germany became a US citizen in 1939. She was a loyal supporter of Allied troops during the war and was awarded the Medal of Freedom by the US government in 1947.*

Above *Dancing in the Rainbow Club in 1945, a London-based club for American servicemen stationed in Britain during the war.*

AT THE MOVIES

Cinema was also extremely popular during the war. In Allied countries, films ranged from newsreels giving brief summaries of important recent events, to cartoons featuring Disney's 'Mickey Mouse' in uniform, and heroic dramas, such as *Destination Tokyo* (United States, 1943) and *In Which We Serve* (UK, 1942). There were also passionate escapist romances such as Hollywood's *Gone With the Wind* (1939), and chronicles of civilian life, for example, *Since You Went Away* (United States, 1944).

Some Hollywood movies boldly satirised Hitler and Nazi Germany and, to a lesser extent, Japan, even before the United States entered the war following the attack on Pearl Harbor in December 1941. Top comedian Charlie Chaplin brilliantly ridiculed Hitler in the feature-length *The Great Dictator* (United States, 1940). That film was preceded by a lesser-known "short subject" by The Three Stooges called *You Nazty Spy* (United States, 1940), in which Moe Howard does the first cinematic impression of Hitler. The Three Stooges (all of whom were Jewish and keenly aware of the Nazis' persecution of the Jews of Europe) followed up this film with a sequel called *I'll Never Heil Again* (United States, 1941).

In Germany, civilian morale was boosted by films celebrating German troops' past bravery, such as submarine adventure *Morgenrot* (1933). In the Soviet Union, epics like *Alexander Nevsky* (1938) portrayed past Russian patriots defeating German invaders.

TIMELINE
1944-1945

3 DECEMBER 1944
British Home Guard told to stand down from duties.

27 JANUARY 1945
Soviet troops liberate Auschwitz concentration camp.

Below *Charlie Chaplin, dressed as Hitler, stares crazily out of this poster for his film The Great Dictator.*

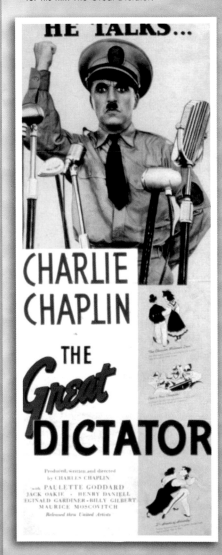

HE TALKS...

CHARLIE CHAPLIN

THE *Great* DICTATOR

Produced, written and directed by CHARLES CHAPLIN
with PAULETTE GODDARD
JACK OAKIE · HENRY DANIELL
REGINALD GARDINER · BILLY GILBERT
MAURICE MOSCOVITCH
Released thru United Artists

Above A British family, holding their gas masks at the ready, listen anxiously to the radio for the latest news of Hitler's threats, 1938.

"We would listen to the radio every night and they would tell you. One particular Sunday night the Germans sunk the 'Wales' and the 'Repulse', which were British ships. When you're listening to it on the radio, it was like it was actually happening. Its very profound to think that this is actually happening somewhere in the world and you're sitting safe in your house."

Katherine O'Grady, a wartime radio listener in the United States, remembers.

Right British journalist Sefton Delmer (1904-1979) broadcasting false information to Germany, 1941. Some propaganda aimed to help and comfort civilians; some was designed to mislead enemies.

HELP FROM THE STARS

Many famous performers, such as Bob Hope from the United States, volunteered to entertain servicemen and women. In Britain, government department ENSA (affectionately nicknamed 'Every Night Something Awful') organised actors, singers, dancers and musicians to tour troop camps in dangerous war zones. Some stars used their fame to speak out against Hitler, including handsome British actor Leslie Howard. He died when his plane was shot down by German aircraft in June 1943.

OVER THE AIRWAVES

In the 1940s, television sets were rare – and in Britain, television was shut down in 1939 at the start of the war – but most families in Europe and the United States had access to a radio. Broadcasting played a vital part in the war effort, uniting listeners and giving them fresh courage. Government leaders appeared on radio regularly; Britain's Winston Churchill became famous for his inspiring speeches. Radio stations also broadcast brisk, cheerful songs to enliven factory workers (mostly played at top volume through loudspeakers) and light-hearted programmes featuring favourite comedians, such as Jack Benny, George Burns and Gracie Allen, Bing Crosby, and Groucho Marx in the United States.

TRUTH AND LIES

Wartime radio reporters sent back the first live, eye-witness, accounts of troop movements or battles. Listeners were thrilled, shocked or deeply moved. In most countries, news bulletins were carefully censored. Only a limited amount of information was released, to avoid

public panic and reduce the risk of revealing useful information to enemies. Some broadcasts were in code, and contained messages to secret agents operating in enemy territory. Others were designed to deceive. British traitor William Joyce (nicknamed 'Lord Haw Haw') spoke by radio from Germany, urging British civilians to surrender. Japanese–American 'Tokyo Rose' made demoralising broadcasts to US troops.

PROPAGANDA

Everywhere, governments used propaganda (messages with a purpose) to encourage, persuade, organise, inform, and, sometimes, command civilians. Propaganda appeared in several formats: radio broadcasts, newspaper articles, films and brightly coloured posters. All featured wartime role models: heroic troops, thrifty housewives, hard-working farm girls, keen factory workers and brave fire-fighters. Governments hoped that these would inspire civilians to work even harder for the war effort. Government propaganda also handed out useful information – such as how to keep pigs, build a bomb-shelter, or stay safe during a poison gas attack. It also warned against idle chatter that might give vital information to enemy spies, reminding civilians that 'careless talk costs lives'.

WARTIME ADVERTISING

Commercial companies liked to include propaganda slogans in their advertisements. They hoped that by linking their products to patriotic themes they would win more customers. Advertisements and propaganda often used humour to get their message across. In Britain, for example, a cartoon character called 'Potato Pete' encouraged children to eat healthy vegetables, and a cartoon monster, called the 'Squanderbug' warned civilians against waste and extravagance.

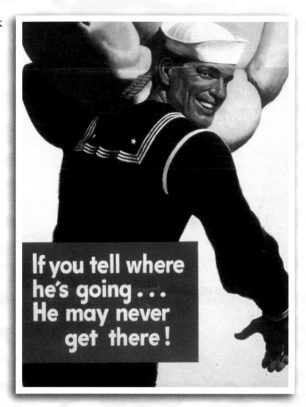

Above *Wartime propaganda warned against discussing troop movements.*

11 FEBRUARY 1945
US President Roosevelt, USSR leader Stalin and UK Prime Minister Churchill meet at Yalta, Ukraine, to plan final attack on Nazis.

13-14 FEBRUARY 1945
British and US planes bomb German city of Dresden.

9 MARCH 1945
US planes fire-bomb Tokyo, Japan, killing 100,000 civilians.

27 MARCH 1945
Last V2 rocket attack on London.

29 MARCH 1945
Last V1 pilotless plane attack in London.

"When der fuehrer says we is de master race,
We heil . . . heil . . . right in der fuehrer's face.
Not to love der fuehrer is a great disgrace,
So we heil . . . heil . . . right in der fuehrer's face.
When Herr Goebbels says we own the world and space,
We heil . . . heil . . . right in Herr Goebbels' face.
When Herr Goering says they'll never bomb dis place,
We heil . . . heil . . . right in Herr Goring's face."

Der Fuehrer's Face, by Spike Jones. Recorded as the theme to Disney's 1943 anti-Nazi propaganda cartoon of the same name, starring Donald Duck. Every mention of "heil" is accompanied by a rude body noise popularly known as a Bronx Cheer.

"In 1943 I arrived in Tehran in Persia [now Iran] on a train from Siberia with thousands of other children, from babies up to age 10. No mothers. No fathers. No adults except for the soldiers.

We were all put into hostels until we could be claimed by someone, or adopted. I didn't speak much but I seemed to be Polish, and so when I was unclaimed the Polish Consul-General and his wife took me and called me 'Magdalena' and I became their daughter.

That is the time when my life started.

I have no recollection before that time."

Magdalena Mokrzycki, one of millions of wartime refugees.

World War II spread devastation round the world on a scale never known before. By 1945, many nations were in ruins. Hundreds of great cities were destroyed. Farms lay abandoned, businesses and industries ceased to operate; governments had huge debts and national economies were in crisis. Worldwide, around 100 million refugees were struggling to survive. There was not enough food, fuel or shelter for them all. How could all the hungry and homeless be looked after? How could battle-scarred troops and exhausted civilians return to normal life?

EMERGENCY AID

International charities, such as the Red Cross, the Red Crescent, and the newly-founded Oxfam, worked valiantly with civilian volunteers to assist refugees. So did Allied troops, thousands of whom were still stationed in Western Europe. But much more help was needed. So, between 1948 and 1951, the United States gave a staggering 13.5 billion dollars in goods and money towards rebuilding Europe. This scheme became known as the 'Marshall Plan' after the US general who managed it. It was generous — but also designed to win support for the United States and its policies. It was rejected by the USSR who did not want to accept the terms offered.

Right *Red Cross nurses and many other voluntary aid workers worked heroically to care for refugees and freed prisoners after the war. Often, no other help was available.*

A NEW BRITAIN

Post-war governments also made ambitious plans. In Britain, for example, the new Socialist government nationalised transport and essential industries, and set up a new 'welfare state' to rid the nation of 'want, disease, ignorance, squalor and idleness'. From 1945, medical care and schooling were free, pensions were introduced, the unemployed got state aid, and mothers were given money to help raise healthy children.

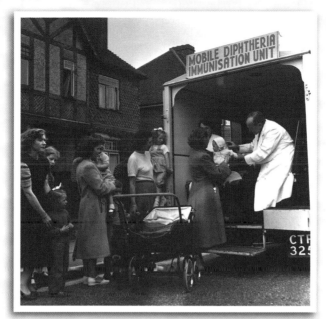

Above In Britain, the new National Health Service launched free mobile mass immunisation services, to combat dangerous infectious diseases.

THE IRON CURTAIN AND OTHER DIVISIONS

Politically, there were still serious problems. Two former wartime allies – and emerging world superpowers – the communist USSR and the capitalist United States, were now bitter rivals. Soviet leader Joseph Stalin had taken control of many Eastern European lands. Churchill famously described the creation of the Soviet bloc of nations as 'an iron curtain' dividing Europe.

It was a curtain that would not rise until the break-up of the Soviet Union into Russia and other independent republics and the general collapse of communism in Eastern Europe in the early 1990s.

"...the United States should do whatever it is able to do to assist in the return of normal economic health in the world, without which there can be no political stability and no assured peace. Our policy is directed not against any country or doctrine but against hunger, poverty, desperation, and chaos. Its purpose should be the revival of a working economy in the world so as to permit the emergence of political and social conditions in which free institutions can exist."

 US General George Marshall outlines the Marshall Plan, 1947.

TIMELINE
1945

24 APRIL 1945
Soviet troops surround Berlin, capital city of Germany.

30 APRIL 1945
Hitler commits suicide in Berlin.

7 MAY 1945
Germany surrenders.

8 MAY 1945
VE (Victory in Europe) Day.

26 JUNE 1945
United Nations is formed.

26 JULY 1945
UK general election: Churchill loses and is replaced as Prime Minister by Clement Attlee.

6 AND 9 AUGUST 1945
United States drops atomic bombs on Japan cities of Hiroshima (August 6) and Nagasaki (August 9).

8 AUGUST 1945
USSR attacks Japanese-occupied Manchuria; 500,000 die, mostly civilians.

14 AUGUST 1945
Japan surrenders.

15 AUGUST 1945
VJ (Victory over Japan) Day.

16 AUGUST 1945
Petrol rationing ends in US.

In 1949 many countries also made alliances with the two post-war superpowers, the United States and the USSR, for extra security. In Western Europe, many joined the North Atlantic Treaty Organization (NATO), led by the Unites States. In Eastern Europe – under communist rule – countries joined the Council for Mutual Economic Assistance (COMECON) and the Warsaw Pact, both led by the USSR.

Above *A ship carrying soldiers from the US 86th Infantry Division docks at New York, 1945, while the men's wives and families wave joyfully from the quayside.*

Below *Carried away! In this famous photo, taken in New York's Time Square, 1945, a US sailor and civilian nurse celebrate Japan's surrender to the Allies.*

"To girls brought up on the cinema, who copied the dress, hair styles and manners of Hollywood film stars, the sudden influx of Americans speaking like the films, who actually lived in the magic country, and who had plenty of money, at once went to the girls' heads. The Americans'... proneness to spoil a girl, to build up, exaggerate, talk big and act with generosity and flamboyance, helped to make them the most attractive of boyfriends."

 British government report, 1945.

THE MIDDLE EAST

In the Middle East, Zionists (Jewish nationalists) and Jewish wartime survivors were struggling to set up a new state, Israel, in a region that was dominated by Arab and other Muslim states. In Asia, colonies ruled by European nations demanded independence. There were power struggles in China, and the divide between communists (backed by the Soviet Union and China) and capitalists (backed by the United States) was threatening peace and stability on the Korean Peninsula. No-one wanted another war, but with new rivalries coming to the surface now that the threat of Nazism had been laid to rest, could war actually be prevented?

ALL TOGETHER

Supported by the Allies, a promising new organisation, the United Nations, was founded on 24 August 1945. Members hoped that future wars could be avoided by diplomacy and maintaining good communication.

Right *The Security Council chamber inside the UN headquarters in New York City. Founded after World War II, its main function is to maintain international peace.*

PEACE AND JOY?

For ordinary civilians, the end of World War II brought joy – at least, to begin with. In Allied countries, celebrating crowds thronged the streets; neighbourhoods held Victory parties. Troops liberating towns and cities from German occupation were warmly welcomed. So were returning servicemen, home safely at last.

However, many families faced a future without husbands and fathers. And many couples, after six years apart, found it hard to adjust to peacetime life together. More happily, many new babies were born in the years after 1945. They soon had a nickname: the 'baby boom' generation. Thousands of G.I. Brides (European women married to US troops) left home to start a new life in the United States.

Women who had worked in well-paid, senior positions in the United States during the war, found that employers preferred returning servicemen, leaving them out of work. There were fewer peacetime jobs open to women, and many were boring and poorly paid. Industries, advertisers and the media all promoted a new image of the ideal female. Her task was to stay at home, keep house, buy consumer goods, and look after children – and men.

TOUGH TIMES

Even with aid from the Marshall Plan, it took years for European nations to repair war damage. In the years just after the war, rationing continued, and some foods were even scarcer than they had been in wartime. Clothes and furnishings were still drab, particularly in the USSR and Soviet-bloc nations. Families still had to share cramped lodgings with relatives or friends. The weather of 1946-1947 was some of the harshest ever experienced. Some refugees still faced starvation. These tough times were known as 'the years of austerity'.

LOOKING AHEAD

Slowly, businesses, industries, professions and public services began to recover. Governments invited men from Africa, Asia and the Caribbean to come to Europe, to work in these new enterprises. Old enemies France and Germany planned a new 'Common Market' (now the European Community). They wanted the nations of Europe to grow prosperous together, and never to fight again.

World War II was over. The home front was a memory. A new future was beginning.

TIMELINE
1945-1948

20 NOVEMBER 1945
Surviving Nazi leaders put on trial for war crimes at Nuremberg, Germany.

23 NOVEMBER 1945
Food rationing (except for sugar) ends in the United States.

7 JUNE 1946
Television broadcasts begin again in Britain.

21 JULY 1946
Bread rationing begins in Britain.

22 JUNE 1948
The ship *Empire Windrush* brings the first post-war immigrant workers to Britain from the Caribbean.

Below *The Empire Windrush arriving at Tilbury docks in in June 1948. Onboard were almost 500 Jamaicans emigrating to England.*

CHAPTER 7

MAJOR FIGURES OUTSTANDING CIVILIANS

World War II was a conflict that engulfed entire continents. It has often been called a war that represented one of the clearest conflicts between forces of evil – the Axis nations led by Hitler's Nazi Germany – and those that would put a stop to that evil – the Allies, which were primarily led by Britain and the United States. Despite the global nature of this conflict, it was in many ways fought not only in the trenches and skies of Europe and the Pacific but in the streets and neighbourhoods as ordinary people tried to keep out of harm's way, help one another to survive, and maintain a sense of their own humanity in the process.

RAOUL WALLENBERG (1912-1947)

Swedish diplomat and businessman Raoul Wallenberg was sent to work in Hungary, an ally of Nazi Germany. He used his diplomatic status to help almost 100,000 Jewish people escape to safety, by issuing documents – which he created himself – giving them permission to travel. He also set up safe houses within Hungary, where Jewish people could safely shelter. He flew Swedish flags outside these refuges, and claimed they were Swedish territory. In 1945, Wallenberg was arrested by Soviet soldiers, advancing into Hungary. They accused him of being a spy. He was never seen again. Later, the Soviet government claimed he died in a Moscow prison, although many feel he may have lived for decades following his arrest.

MORDECAI ANIELEWICZ (1919-1943)

Polish Jewish student Mordecai Anielewicz was born to a poor family. After leaving school, he joined a Jewish youth movement, and proved himself to be an inspiring leader and organiser. Still a teenager, he tried to help Jewish people escape from Poland to Israel, but was caught and put in prison. Once free, he returned to his home city, Warsaw, Poland, to join resistance fighters. In 1943, he learned that the Nazis planned to shut down the Warsaw Ghetto, and send all its inhabitants to concentration camps. The Jews in the ghetto were outnumbered by Nazi troops, and had no chance of surviving, but they battled bravely for four weeks, led by Anielewicz. They refused to surrender even after he was killed.

JEAN MOULIN (1899-1943)

French government official Jean Moulin refused to obey unjust orders from Nazis in occupied France. So, in 1940, he was dismissed from his job, and decided to join the French Resistance. He spent the rest of his life in disguise and on the run. In 1943, Moulin made a top secret journey to Britain, where General Charles de Gaulle, leader of the exiled Free French forces, trusted him with a very important mission: to organise all the separate resistance groups to work together. Shortly after setting up the National Council of the resistance in 1943, Moulin was captured by the Nazis. He died either from the torture, or by committing suicide, but never betrayed his comrades.

HENRY J. KAISER (1882-1967)

Until World War II, American Henry J. Kaiser had been involved in building bridges, dams and roads. After the United States entered World War II however, Kaiser used his political influence to win competitive ship-building contracts. Using prefabricated parts and assembly-line techniques in an industry unfamiliar with either, Kaiser's methods focused on speed rather than quality. In this way, Kaiser managed to cut the average time taken to produce a Liberty ship – a basic cargo ship – from 355 days to just 56 days. By the end of the war, Kaiser's shipyards had built more than one-third of all US ships launched during the conflict.

MINNIE VAUTRIN (1886-1941)

Born and educated in the United States, Minnie Vautrin sailed to China in 1912 to work as a teacher and Christian missionary. She helped set up and run a school and college for girls at Nanking. When the Japanese army invaded Nanking in 1937, Vautrin worked with others to turn the college into a refuge for 10,000 women and girls fleeing Japanese invaders. In spite of heroically saving so many defenceless people, Vautrin was haunted by all those whom she had not managed to help. She wrote, 'There is probably no crime that has not been committed in this city.' Overwhelmed with horror and disgust at the brutality she had seen, Vautrin committed suicide at home in Illinois.

ANNE FRANK (1929-1945)

The teenage daughter of a German Jewish family, Anne Frank fled with her parents and sister to Amsterdam in the Netherlands. After the Nazis invaded in 1940, they all went into hiding until August 1944. Then they were betrayed, arrested, and sent to a concentration camp along with over 1000 other Jews from the Netherlands. Anne died from typhus, aged 15, in March 1945. While Anne was in hiding, she kept a diary describing her fears and frustrations, and her hopes for the future. It was published after the war ended, and became famous world-wide as a symbol of one girl's enduring faith in herself – and in humanity.

JOZEF ULM (1900-1944)
WIKTORIA ULM (1912-1944)

Jozef and Wiktoria Ulm were farmers, living in a peaceful village in south-east Poland. When the war started, they agreed to hide eight Jewish civilians from a nearby community, even though sheltering Jews was automatically punished by death in occupied Poland. In 1944, a suspicious policeman arranged for the Ulms' house to be searched by German soldiers. First, the Jewish hideaways were discovered and shot, then Josef and Wiktoria (who was pregnant). When the six young Ulm children saw their parents being killed, they started crying and shouting in terror. To silence them, the policeman and the Nazi soldiers brutally killed them all.

CHARITY BICK (1925 [OR 1927]-2002)

Bomb-raid heroine Charity Bick lied about her age and joined the UK Air Raid Precautions volunteers aged only 14. She served as a despatch rider (bicycle messenger). In 1941, she climbed onto a roof to help extinguish a lethal incendiary bomb, then cycled four times through gunfire and falling bombs to carry urgent messages. For her courage and determination, Bick was awarded the George Cross, Britain's highest civilian medal. She was the youngest person ever to receive it.

VERA CHALBUR (born 1914-disappeared 1940)

German spy Vera Chalbur was born to Jewish parents, and worked as a night-club dancer in Paris, France. She became friendly with top German secret agents, and was recruited as a spy. Her beauty, charm, bravery and intelligence made her very successful. In 1940, Chalbur was parachuted into Scotland on a secret mission, together with two colleagues. They were all arrested. Chalbur's comrades were executed, but Chalbur disappeared. Historians think that she changed sides and began spying for Britain, helping to defeat the Nazis, but her full story is still secret.

DR CHARLES R. DREW (1904-1950)

African-American doctor, researcher and athlete Charles R. Drew was an expert in blood transfusion procedures. He worked to improve techniques used for blood transfusions, safety checking, and storage. He set up the first-ever 'blood banks', to hold large stocks of blood ready to treat injured soldiers and emergency workers. He also campaigned to end racial segregation of blood supplied by donors. In 1940, he played a leading part in the 'Blood for Britain' project, set up to treat British troop and civilian casualties at the start of World War II. His work saved countless lives.

Members of the Women's Voluntary Service, killed in action 1938-1945

Founded in 1938 in the UK, the 'Women's Voluntary Service for Air Raid Precautions' was staffed by female volunteers, and dedicated to helping civilians. In 1939, members helped evacuate over a million children from big cities. They also ran hostels, clubs, community feeding centres, first-aid posts and mother-and-baby clubs. They welcomed and cared for refugees, ran emergency clothing stores, made camouflage nets, handed out ration books and provided transport for hospital patients. By 1941, the WVS had a million members. They continued to help those in need during the most dangerous bombing raids and fires. Many WVS members were awarded medals for bravery; 241 were killed in action.

GLOSSARY

Allies The nations who declared war on Nazi Germany in 1939, including Britain, France and Poland. The Allies were aided by their colonies and dominions in India, southern Africa, the Caribbean, Canada, Australia and New Zealand, and joined later by the United States and USSR.

Anschluss The German word for 'union'. In the build-up to World War II it was used to describe the forced union of Nazi Germany and Austria.

Anti-Semitic Hatred of and discrimination against Jews.

Appease Used to describe the efforts by British governments in the 1930s to avoid war with Germany.

ARP Air Raid Precautions. The name given to several organised groups of volunteers in Britain who served bravely on the home front.

Axis Powers The initial alliance of Germany and Italy in 1936, later including Japan and other nations that opposed the Allies in World War II.

Billeted Sent to live in a particular place, on the orders of a government or military authorities.

Black-out Measures to stop visible light from houses, shops, factories, street-lights and all kinds of transport escaping into the night sky and helping to guide enemy bombers to their targets. Also referred to as 'dim-out'.

Blitz The German word for 'lightning'. Used during World War II to describe the intensive bombing raids on London.

Blitzkrieg The German term meaning 'lightning war'.

Bloc Group of nations sharing the same political aims or following the same leader. Used to describe the group of nations in Eastern Europe allied with the USSR after World War II (Soviet Bloc).

Capitalist Supporting political ideas that include freedom for individuals and corporations to own and run businesses, make profits and create wealth.

Cartridges Attachments at the base of bullets. They are packed with explosives to shoot the bullet.

Chancellor Elected leader of a government. Used to describe Adolf Hitler's position as the leader of Germany.

Civilians Men, women and children who do not belong to any of the armed forces.

Communist Followers of writer Karl Marx who believe that the state should own all property, and run businesses, industries, schools, hospitals and other institutions.

Concentration camp A prison camp for people whom the authorities wish to remove or separate from society.

Conscientious objectors Citizens who refuse to fight because of religious or ethical beliefs.

Conscripted Forced by law to join an army, navy, air-force or other wartime service.

Doctrine Belief or set of ideas.

Einzatsgruppen Mobile killing squads; Nazi troops sent to execute Jewish communities in north and east Europe.

Evacuated Sent away from home to escape the danger of enemy attack.

Fire-watchers Civilian volunteers who kept lookout during bombing raids, especially for signs of fire caused by incendiaries or other bombs.

Gasket Thin layer of compressible material fitted between two parts of a metal joint to seal it and prevent leakage.

Ghetto Closed-off neighbourhood where living conditions are poor. Usually, ghettoes are home to oppressed or minority communities. In Nazi-occupied Europe during World War II, thousands of Jewish people were forced to live in ghettoes.

Great Depression Worldwide economic crisis that began in 1929 and lasted for most of the 1930s.

Holocaust Name given by historians to the organised mass slaughter of Jews and other civilian groups by the Nazis.

Incendiaries Bombs full of chemicals that catch fire when they hit their target and burn very fiercely.

Interned Imprisoned without trial.

Kindertransport Organised movement of Jewish children out of Nazi-occupied lands to safety at the start of World War II. The children's parents were not allowed to travel with them; most of these parents later died.

Mobilised Made ready to fight.

Nazi (National Socialist German Workers') Party Founded in January 1919, it was based on militaristic, racial, anti-Semitic and nationalistic policies.

Neutral Not taking part in a war.

Occupation The invasion and take-over of one country by another, enemy nation.

Pearl Harbor A US naval base in Hawaii which Japan attacked without warning on 7 December 1941. Much of the US Pacific fleet was destroyed and the incident led to the United States entry into World War II.

Propaganda Media (such as books, newspapers, posters, broadcasts, advertisements, films and songs) with a political message.

Radiation sickness Very serious illness caused by radiation from atomic weapons or other radioactive sources. Symptoms include sickness, weakness, extreme fatigue, lowered resistance to infection and a high risk of developing cancer.

Renovation Repairing an object and making it look new.

Resigned Accepting a situation without complaint or protest.

Socialist Someone who believes that the state should take control of society, run the economy, and limit the powers and profits of rich individuals and businesses.

Squalor Conditions including dirt, filth, poverty and often corruption.

Sullen Sulky; angry, silent and withdrawn.

Superpower An extremely powerful state. After the end of World War II, there were only two world superpowers, the United States and the USSR.

Tacker Shipyard worker who helped prepare metal parts for welders.

Thrifty Keen to save money and avoid waste.

Torpedoed Hit (and often sunk) by an underwater bomb, called a torpedo.

U-boats Name, in English, given to German submarines. 'U' stands for the German word *untersee*, which means 'under sea'.

USSR The Union of Soviet Socialist Republics; a nation founded after a Communist revolution in Russia in 1917. It was made up of many nations, or republics, in Eastern Europe and Central Asia, stretching from the Baltic Sea to the borders of China. The USSR supported other communist states all round the world.

Welfare State A collection of services, such as health-care and pensions, run by governments, paid for by taxes, and designed to care for citizens throughout their lives. In Britain, the Welfare State was planned by British political leaders during World War II, and introduced after the war ended.

Zionists Jewish nationalists who aimed to build a new Jewish state, Israel.

INDEX

ACKNOWLEDGEMENTS

PICTURE CREDITS:

Every effort has been made to trace the copyright holders, and we apologise in advance for any unintentional ommissions. We would be pleased to insert the appropriate acknowledgements in any subsequent edition of this publication.

B=bottom; C=centre; L=left; R=right; T=top

20th C.Fox/Everett/Rex Features: 33br. AElfwine/ Wikimedia Commons: 18b. age fotostock/ SuperStock: 24t. From *American Goddess at the Rape of Nanking: The Courage of Minnie Vautrin by Hua-ling Hu* (Southern Illinois University Press, 2000): 41b. Archive of Mateusz Szpytma: 42tr. Miquel Benitez/Rex Features: 17b. Bentley Archive/Popperfoto/Getty Images: 10t. Bettmann/CORBIS: OFCb, 2, 12b, 15t, 24b, 25b, 37b, 38t. British Government/Wikimedia Commons: OBCtl. Corbis: 30t. CSU Archives/Everett Collection/Rex Features: 5t. Paul Broadbent/Alamy: 30b. epa/Corbis: 40tl. Everett Collection/Rex Features: 43tr. David J. & Janice L. Frent Collection/Corbis: 4br. Getty Images: 9b, 10b, 11t, 16, 17t, 20b, 21, 22t, 23, 26b, 27t, 29t, 29b, 31b, 32-33, 33t, 34b, 26b, 39b, 41tl, 43b. Hulton-Deutsch Collection/CORBIS: 13t, 22b, OFCtr, OBC(background). The Illustrated London News Picture Library, London, UK/The Bridgeman Art Library: 18t. Imperial War Museum 28b, 42b. iStock: OBCbr, 6b, 16b, 27b. Mary Evans Picture Library/ Alamy: 13b. Minnesota Historical Society/CORBIS: OFCtl. The National Archives: 43tl. National Archives and Records Administration: 19b. Popperfoto/Getty Images: 6t, 10-11, 12t, 34t, 37t. Private Collection/Look and Learn/The Bridgeman Art Library: 14b, 19t. Private Collection/Peter Newark Historical Pictures/The Bridgeman Art Library: 20t. Rex Features: 4bl, 42tl. Roger-Viollet/Rex Features: 5b. Shutterstock: OBCtr, bl, 4-5(background), 6-7(background), 6b, 39t, 48. SNAP/Rex Features: 32t. Swim Ink 2, LLC/CORBIS: 8t, 26t, 31t. ticktock Media Archive: 4t. Time & Life Pictures/Getty Images: 7t, 35t, 38br. Underwood & Underwood/CORBIS: 8b. United States Navy: 41tr. Wikimedia Commons: 40r.